Sheila Leeds

Martin Zender is known as The World's Most Outspoken Bible Scholar. He is an essayist, conference speaker, radio personality, humorist, and the author of several books on spiritual freedom. His essays have appeared in the *Chicago Tribune*, the *Atlanta Journal-Constitution*, the *Cleveland Plain Dealer*, and other newspapers. He has hosted the Grace Café radio program at WCCD in Cleveland, and the syndicated Zender/Sheridan Show at flagship station WBRI in Indianapolis.

www.martinzender.com

Eve Raised

Also by Martin Zender

EVE RAISED

Why women think the apostle Paul
doesn't like them.

Starke & Hartmann, Inc.

Eve Raised

© 2018 by Martin Zender

Published by Starke & Hartmann
P.O. Box 6473
Canton, OH 44706
www.starkehartmann.com
1-866-866-BOOK

Printed in the United States of
America

ISBN-13: 978-0-9842548-7-3
ISBN-10: 0-9842548-7-0

Photo credits: The following photos © Can Stock Photo: Cover photo and pg. 7: Mark2121; pg. 25: nastia 1983; pg. 53: lisafx; pg. 56: Vegas; pg. 76: luisafer.

The following photos: flickr.com, attribution only (https://creativecommons.org/licenses/by/2.0/): pg. 17: dno 1967 b; pg. 22: Cia de Foto 1; pg. 29: bobster855; pg. 37: bobster855; pg. 40: payalnic; pg. 41: GallivangingGirl; dTDesign Photography; pg. 60: jimmysudekum; pg. 64: high SPF by popo-fatticus; pg. 70: benandbarnet.

To Hannah Brook May

"The woman is the glory
of the man."

—*the apostle Paul*
1 Corinthians 11:7

Though historically known as the better sex, women have suffered year upon end of slight and degradation. It seems to have begun in the beginning. Created after man and deceived in Eden, woman later receives this trilogy of "blessing" from the apostle Paul:

- "Be subject to your husband."
- "Be quiet in church."
- "Save yourself by having babies."

In a John Lennon song from the early seventies, the ex-Beatle refers to woman as "the slave of the slaves." Helen Reddy tried looking the other way by singing, "I am strong. I am invincible." Women are caught in a crossfire between the desire to serve others and the need to possess some semblance of independence and self-respect. These two desires, however, seem mutually exclusive.

Women in quietness

Here is a passage from the apostle Paul that has disheartened women for two millennia and made men think more highly of themselves than they ought:

> Let a woman be learning in quietness with all subjection. Now I am not permitting a woman to be teaching, nor yet to be domineering over a man, but to be in quietness (for Adam was first molded, thereafter Eve, and Adam was not seduced, yet the woman, being deluded, has come to be in the transgression). Yet she shall be saved through the child bearing, if ever they should be remaining in faith and love and holiness with sanity.
>
> —*1 Timothy 2:11-15*

I have seen entire books attempting to explain this passage. This is also an entire book, albeit 200 pages shorter than most.

Obviously, women are able to teach. We need only consider Priscilla who, with her husband

Aquila, took the great teacher Apollos aside and expounded the way of God to him more accurately (Acts 18:26). But this was on-the-side instruction, apart from the formal gathering. In the above passage from 1 Timothy, Paul refers to an official role within the ecclesia, or church. In the very next chapter Paul writes: "These things I am writing to you . . . that you may be perceiving how one must behave in God's house, which is the ecclesia of the living God" (1 Timothy 3:15).

1 Corinthians 14:34,35 confirms this:

> Let the women in the ecclesias hush, for it is not permitted to them to speak, but let them be subject, according as the law, also, is saying. Now, if they want to learn anything, let them be inquiring of their own husbands at home, for it is a shame for a woman to be speaking in the ecclesia.

In the 1 Timothy passage, Paul explains why he forbids women to teach:

> For Adam was first molded, thereafter Eve, and Adam was not seduced, yet the woman, being deluded, has come to be in the transgression.

What is the point of stating Adam's primacy? Why would that keep a woman from teaching? Does "second" equal "second rate?" Was Eve less intelligent because she came later? Is that why she can't teach? Can she not teach because she's dumber than the male? Less accomplished? More prone to do evil? We are subtly—if not overtly—led to believe these things. If such things are true based solely on order of appearance, then why was Abel wiser than Cain? Why did the second-born please God while the firstborn committed murder? If second human equals second-*rate* human, then why, in 1 Corinthians 11:7, does Paul call woman "the glory of the man?" This anticipates a later point, but it serves us now.

Glory

The word "glory," in the Greek, is *doxa*. Its literal element is "SEEM." (See page 124 of Greek-English Keyword Concordance in the *Concordant Literal New Testament*.) The definition is "a highly favorable opinion and that which impresses it on the senses or the mind."

Here is the 1 Corinthians passage in context:

For a man, indeed, ought not to be covering his head, being inherently the image and glory of

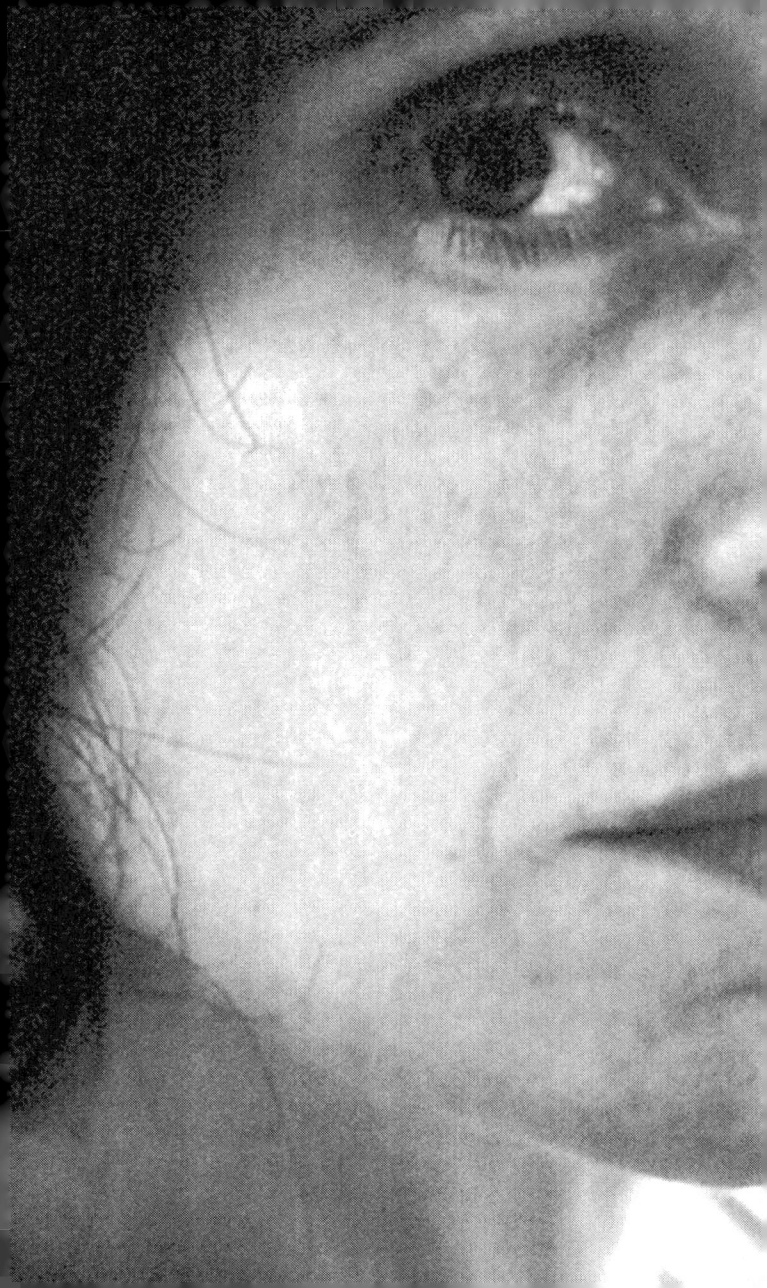

God. Yet the woman is the glory of the man.
For man is not out of woman, but woman out
of man.

—*1 Corinthians 11:7-8*

God is invisible (1 Timothy 1:17). To be
known and appreciated by sensate creatures, He
must be represented in the visible realm. His
best representation in the universe is the human
race, specifically, the only perfect specimen *of* this
race—our Lord Jesus Christ. In the days of His
flesh here on Earth, our Lord gave those with eyes
and ears a highly favorable opinion of God. Thus,
He was the glory of God. He was also a male, and
still is. It is in this sense—the sense that a man is
a member of the race that produced Christ—that
any male besides Christ can be said to be God's
glory.

Where does this leave females? Are they not
the image and glory of God? I will let Scripture
answer that question:

So Elohim created humanity in His image; in
the image of Elohim He created it: male and
female He created them.

—*Genesis 1:27, Concordant
Version of the Old Testament*

Women, too, are created in the image of God. Therefore they, as well as men, are God's glory. 1 Corinthians 11:7-8 is telling us something *else* that a woman is. Not only is a woman the image and glory of God, she is also the glory of the man. She has a dual glory.

Again, God required glory so that sensate creatures could think favorably of Him. We easily grasp God's reason for this: He's invisible. Why does a male require glory? Can't he already be seen? There must be something else the male lacks. What is the male lacking that, without the female, would lend to any onlooker an unfavorable opinion of humanity? Only four things that I can think of off the top of my head: 1) grace, 2) beauty, 3) kindness, and 4) mercy.

I do not mean to say that males lack these qualities *in toto,* but that females tend to possess these qualities more than males, making them shine forth like the sun's corona. A woman standing next to a man gives the universe a better impression of that man than would be otherwise possible. The woman of Proverbs 31 demonstrates this. Her talents, to her gender, are God-placed.

I cite here the verbs credited to the Proverbs wife, and then contrast them with those native to the husband:

WIFE—seeks (vs. 13), works (13), brings (14), rises (15), provides (15), plans (16), girds (17), makes (17), inspects (18), puts forth (19), spreads (20), produces (24), watches (27)

HUSBAND—sits (23)

Some wives among my readers are thinking to themselves, *yes; that's about right.* In quick defense of the husband, he is not sitting on a La-Z-Boy recliner. "Her spouse is acknowledged in the gateways, when he sits with the elders of the land" (Proverbs. 31:23). The husband occupies an esteemed place in the community. How did he get there? Her.

The last verse of this chapter, verse 31, reads: "Give honor to her for the fruit of her hands, and let them praise her in the gateways for her deeds."

In the very same place where her husband sits, the wife is honored for the fruit of her hands and is praised for her deeds. My conclusion: *he* is the fruit of her hands; *he* is one of her deeds. He is glorified in the gates because of her. Because of the many verbs she executes on his behalf, he is acknowledged. His glory is not his own; *she* fostered and nourished it.

"Her spouse's heart puts trust in her, so that he lacks no proceeds" (vs. 11). The husband's proceeds are of her. In a sense, she *is* the proceeds. His glory results from what she has accomplished. She is his glory.

"She rises while it is still night and provides food for her household" (vs. 15). Women possess an endurance men don't have. The Proverbs 31 woman multitasks, even before the sun. Men cannot successfully do this. Men can do only one thing well at a time; they can do two or three things badly. Males lack glory. They cannot generally provide for themselves a favorable opinion. This glory, this favorable opinion, is provided for them by the female. The female is their glory.

A male without a female rarely realizes his potential.

"She spreads out her palm to the humbled and puts forth her hands to the needy" (vs. 20). The most humble and needy among us are babies and children. Women not only further the race, they feed it, clothe it, and send it to school. Then they spread out their palms to other humbled and needy people, such as the sick and elderly. More women are nurses than men. Why? Women simply care more about sick people. Women fix the people that men hurt. Women, not men, send cards to the ailing. They

send cards to the afflicted, and to those deserving praise. They send cards to sick people, to the wedded, to the graduated, to anniversary people, and to the families of the dead. Were it not for women, Hallmark would be out of business by the end of the month.

"She makes decorative covers for herself; her clothing is cambric and purple" (vs. 22).

The only other reference to "decorative covers" in Scripture is Proverbs 7:16-17. The seductress says to her suitor, "I have decorated my divan with decorative covers, with bedspreads of Egyptian yarn. I have wafted my bed with myrrh, aloes and cinnamon." Whatever they touch, women beautify. If something is decorated, a female did it. Wherever pleasant odors waft, do not seek the responsible male. You will not find him. He does not exist.

Females, not males, beautify themselves. Within them lies the potential for Godlike comeliness. It is Esther, not Mordecai, and not King Ahasuerus, who indulges in "oil of myrrh," "aromatics" and "beauty-treatments of the women" (Esther 2:12). The phrase "beauty-treatments of the men," in Scripture, is not to be found. It is not that men are already fair while women are not. Rather, men cannot be helped. Women possess a mysterious capability—an exclusive potential unknown to the opposing gender—to enhance their appearance. Already beautiful, they can be rendered sublime. From wells deep within them can be coaxed near-visions of God. Woman is God's testimony, on Earth, that *He* is beautiful.

Because of woman, our species takes away the collective breath of the universe. In form and in face—truly—females are our glory. When the New Jerusalem descends from heaven, it does not please the spirit to compare it to a male—

> And I perceived the holy city, New Jerusalem, descending out of heaven from God, made ready as a bride adorned for her husband.
> —*Revelation 21:2*

Women, not men, are adorned. Grace be upon all women. As the sun antedates its effulgence, so does Adam antedate *his* glory. As the cut diamond emerges from the rough, so does Eve succeed the first human—

> The woman is the glory of the man. For man is not out of woman, but woman out of man.
> —*1 Corinthians 11:7-8*

Woman, coming second, is not least. Glory, by nature, comes out of that which it glorifies.

Glory cherished

The source of glory cherishes that which glorifies it, and indeed, is beholden to do so. Thus, man cherishes woman; husbands cherish wives; parents cherish children; God cherishes Christ. But isn't the obverse also true? Does not glory cherish its source? Yes, but not to the same degree. How can it? It hasn't the contrast of absence. Eve never knew the pang of aloneness, and neither did Christ—until the cross. Parents cannot imagine life without their children. Children began life with parents. They take them for granted—until they're gone.

In the case of Christ, God delivered to death that which He cherished most. Husbands are *not* to be imitators of God in this respect! Husbands, rather, are called upon to nurture and cherish their wives; to feed, clothe, protect and love them.

> Husbands, be loving your wives according as Christ also loves the ecclesia, and gives Himself up for its sake . . . For no one at any time hates his own flesh, but is nurturing and cherishing it, according as Christ also the ecclesia.
> —*Ephesians 5:25,29*

Scriptural precedent dictates that the first sacrifice for the subsequent. In a world of sin, this ideal is not always enacted (as with Jacob and Esau, and Joseph and his brothers), but it remains the ideal. Thus, Abram risks his own life to rescue Lot (Genesis 14:14-15); Moses faces the thunder and lightning of Sinai for Israel's sake, later interceding on the nation's behalf (Exodus 32:9-11); David laments the death of his son, crying out: "Oh, my son Absolom! Would I had died instead of you!" (2 Samuel 18:33); Paul, the first member of the body of Christ, writes, "I am suffering evil unto bonds as a malefactor . . . I am enduring all *because of those who are chosen*, that they also may be happening upon the salvation which is in Christ Jesus with glory eonian" (2 Timothy 2:9-10).

Adam, as a figure of Christ, embodies this same spirit. Because the serpent deluded Eve and not him, he knowingly partakes of the fruit to accompany his wife through the veil (and the vale) of sin and death.

These things being said, why would men, being first, expose their glory to the perils of public teaching? They should not. Such a thing would be a shame.

Subjection to protection
In Paul's second letter to Timothy, the apostle calls his spiritual son to a life of teaching:

And what things you hear from me through many witnesses, these commit to faithful men, who shall be competent to teach others also.
—2 Timothy 2:2

He immediately follows with:

Suffer evil with me, as an ideal soldier of Christ Jesus.   *—2 Timothy 2:3*

Paul equates teaching with warfare and suffering, and teachers with frontline warriors. And well he should. Paul, a frontline warrior himself, was shipwrecked, flogged, stoned, consigned to a swamp, left naked and shivering, and lowered from the Damascus wall in a basket to escape assassins (2 Corinthians 11:23-28)—all due to teaching. Do we really want to see these things happening to Priscilla? *Do* we?

"Let a woman be learning in quietness with all subjection. Now I am not permitting a woman to be teaching" (1 Timothy 2:11-12).

Nothing is too good for the glory of the man, that is, for the woman. Her subjection to the man (who seeks to spare her) is her protection. His desire to subject her in this matter is a gift to her. She may want to teach and be quite able for the task, but instead subjects herself to the

man for her own good. The man has a better assessment of her value than she does. Where she would endanger and waste herself (for she is blinded by her own talent and ambition), he says, "No. I will not allow you. I will spare you."

The ecclesia did the same for Paul in Acts, chapter 19. The silversmiths of Ephesus had enriched themselves selling handmade silver images of Artemis, goddess of the Ephesians. In Acts 19 they are in full riot on the heels of Paul's unpopular statement, "They are not gods which are coming into being by means of hands." The silversmiths "rush with one accord into the theater, gripping Agius and Aristachus, Macedonians, fellow travelers of Paul" (vs. 29).

Hearing of this, Paul's first impulse is to venture into the theater. *Who better than me*, thinks Paul, *to explain my motives, placate the silversmiths, and probably save some of the throng through the heralding of the evangel?* And yet, if Paul ventures into this theater, there will *be* no heralding of the evangel; the rioters will tear him to pieces. Paul is blinded to this reality by his own ambition, and is saved from it by his friends:

> Now, at Paul's intending to enter into the populace, the disciples did not let him. Yet some of the chiefs of the province of Asia, also, being

his friends, sending to him, entreated him not to venture into the theater himself.

—*Acts 19:30-31*

It was friends, not enemies, who kept Paul from the mob, subjecting him to their will. The friends might have said to the apostle (I am adapting this from 1 Timothy 2:11-15):

Let yourself be hushed, Paul. We are not permitting you to speak. Be subject to us, in this matter. It would be a shame for you to be speaking to this dangerous ecclesia. We are not permitting you to be domineering over us in this matter. We know how capable you are; your inclination to domineer springs from your ability, we know this. But please be in quietness. Do not let this enemy either hear or see you. You shall be saved through this trial if ever you should be remaining in our advice, with faith and love and holiness with sanity.

What happened next?

Now after the tumult ceased, Paul, sending after the disciples and consoling and saluting them, came away to go into Macedonia. Now, passing through those parts and entreating

them with many a word, he came into Greece
. . . Now it was arranged for him to be met,
as far away as the province of Asia, by Sopater
Pyrrhus, a Berean, yet of the Thessalonians,
Aristarchus and Secundus, and Gaius the
Berbian, and Timothy, yet of the province of
Asia, Tychicus and Trophimus. Now these,
coming before, remained for us in Troas.
Yet we sail off from Philippi after the days of
unleavened bread, and came to them in Troas
in five days, where we tarry seven days.
                                   —*Acts 20:1-2,4-6*

Paul first of all consoled and saluted the
disciples who had saved him. Why would they
require consolation? They had kept Paul from
doing his duty, or what he thought was his duty.
They had dared to confront the great apostle.
They put their foot down: "You have persuaded
us before, Paul. But not this time." In this calm
after the storm, they might have feared apostolic
retribution. The same calm, however, turns Paul
reflective. He realizes that they had been right.
Not only does he console them, he salutes them.

The Greek word translated "salute" in the
Concordant Literal New Testament is *aspazomai*.
The two elements of this word are "simultane-
ous" and "pull." Like this: *simultaneous-pull*.

What a picturesque word for "hug."

My goal in writing is not only to tell the truth, but to cause that truth to soothe and heal hurt feelings between the genders. The misconstruing of Paul's "women can't teach" passages have turned women not only against God and Paul, but against men. Some men have deserved it. They have treated women—at least in their attitudes—as second-class saints. These passages, to men, have become text-weapons with which to belittle the female rather than protect and cherish her. The males, flattering themselves, read Paul's words and crown themselves kings. Strange. These passages, rightly grasped, make the men dedicated guardians of the fair sex.

Let us together-pull—men and women—with new understanding.

After he is spared, Paul greets and entreats his close acquaintances. Following the Ephesian melee, Paul is met by Sopater, Aristarchus, Secundus, Gaius, Timothy, Tychicus, and Trophimus. These are the good guys; women are no doubt on the periphery. Paul was never happier than when sharing God's greater graces with beloved acquaintances. I hinted earlier at Priscilla's teaching ministry to that godly man, Apollos. She and her husband took a teachable soul to themselves and expounded the way of

God to him more accurately. Read the account for yourself in Acts 18:24-26. Again, women are best suited, not to the breaking of ice, but to the molding of ice—already broken—into beautiful sculpture.

Quietness the ideal

And so: "Let a woman be learning in quietness." This is not the quietness of "shut up," but the quietness of "be at peace; be hushed." In the same context, Paul writes:

> I am entreating, then, first of all, that petitions, prayers, pleadings, thanksgiving be made for all humanity, for kings and all those being in a superior station, *that we may be leading a mild and quiet life in all devoutness and gravity, for this is ideal and welcome in the sight of our Savior, God.*   —1 Timothy 2:1-3

Did Paul live a mild and quiet life? Hardly. A teacher—especially a teacher of grace in an era of Judaizers—was unlikely to live either mildly or quietly. Thus, the teacher does not lead the ideal life. This is one reason James says in James 3:1, "Not many should become teachers, my brethren, being aware that we shall be getting greater judgment."

A teacher puts his neck on the line, both in this life and in the next.

Women, as we have seen, are our better selves. It is our duty to keep them from struggle and harm. They are too precious to be exposed, challenged, shot at, stoned, tortured, shipwrecked, and raped. Why not spare the sons of Adam, that is, males? Because Adam was first molded, thereafter Eve. He is the expendable one; the one of whom we require this kind of sacrifice. The woman is his glory, and her we must preserve.

What nation sends its women to the front lines of wars? Any civilization worthy of the name protects its women and children from armed conflict for the same reason the Smithsonian protects the Hope Diamond. Is it that the Hope Diamond is not good enough to mingle with the other rocks? No. It's *too* good; it's *too* precious. It belongs to a more esteemed category than the other rocks.

The apostle Peter also wishes for women, "a meek and quiet spirit, which, in God's sight, is costly" (1 Peter 3:4). Would that more women wished the same for themselves—and that more men wished to provide it. A quiet life is a promotion; it is an *upgrade* from teaching. It is more *costly* than teaching.

We miss the import of 1 Timothy 2:12 by mistaking teaching for the ideal life. It is hardly that. Rather, it is a life fraught with mental, spiritual, and physical perils. When we appraise teaching in this new light, new light dawns. Paul wants females ducked into the relative safety of the trench. "Be quiet," he says. "Hush." *He must be worried that the women will say something stupid and embarrass the men*. No; that's our modern interpretation; that's *our* opinion of women. Paul wants women protected; undetected. Protected and undetected by whom? By the prince of darkness himself.

> Now a slave of the Lord must not be fighting, but be gentle toward all, apt to teach, bearing with evil, with meekness training those who are antagonizing, seeing whether God may be giving them repentance to come into a realization of the truth, and they will be sobering up out of the trap of the Adversary, having been caught alive by him, for that one's will.
> —*2 Timothy 2:24-26*

Shall we cast our fair sex into the arena of evil to wrestle Satan? Rather, let us protect it. Let us cherish women and bestow upon them peace and quiet, that they may lead the ideal life,

which is costly. Costly to whom? To men. Let *us* fight on their behalf, and die for them defending truth, if necessary. Let them teach privately and peacefully, as did Priscilla, discerning in the likes of Apollos a teachable spirit. Let women eluci-date the riches of Christ's grace, one-on-one, to those primed by God to receive their wisdom. Let us neither ask them nor allow them to break down stone walls of unbelief. Let us neither ask them nor allow them to face the antagonism that accompanies public discourse. To do either thing would be to expose our glory to Satanic fury. This is no melodrama. The religious world is infested with "the teachings of demons" (1 Timothy 4:1).

The public teacher, with Scriptural argument, fights Satan. His goal is to save his hearers from deception. Our Lord Jesus Christ also fought Satan, from the cross, with the goal of saving sinners from death. Christ's relationship to the ecclesia provides a parallel example of a man's relationship to a woman—and a husband's rela-tionship to a wife—in reference to protection and duty:

I am not permitting the ecclesia to be going to the cross, nor yet to be domineering over Christ, but to be in quietness, (for Christ was first molded, there-

after the ecclesia, and Christ was not seduced, yet the ecclesia, being deluded, has come to be in the transgression).

It is clear to see, in this example, the gift of a) "I am not permitting you," and b) "be in quietness." Who among us would want to face Calvary? Who among us, in that awful hour, would not welcome the comforting words of Christ: "No. You stay here. *I* will go. For I was first molded, thereafter you. I know Satan; he will seduce you. You cannot withstand him. Me, he has never deceived. Remain here; be in quietness. Rest. *I* was first molded; I am the responsible One. I will win this battle—*for your sake.*"

Deceived in innocence

"Adam was not seduced, yet the woman, being deluded, has come to be in the transgression" (1 Timothy 2:14). Here it is, then: Adam's primacy lent him an awareness Eve lacked. Adam knew every beast—including the serpent—long before God molded Eve. By the time Eve arrived, Adam had appraised and named every creature (Genesis 2:19).

Some modern interpreters contend that women, being latecomers, should not teach

because they're gullible; they haven't been around; they're new to the game; they don't know the rules. That Eve was new to the game is true. She knew the rules, yes, but she missed the PowerPoint presentation on Satan's subtlety. She thought better of creation. She trusted it more explicitly than did Adam. Here is another reason why women should not teach publicly in the ecclesia: they too easily trust. That women should not teach because they're gullible is wrong; it's too negative of a slant.

Women should not teach...*because they're innocent.*

> Now I am entreating you, brethren, to be noting those who are making dissensions and snares beside the teaching which you learned, and avoid them, for such for our Lord Christ are not slaving, but for their own bowels, *and through compliments and adulation are deluding the hearts of the innocent.* —Romans 16:17-18

Adam was innocent, yes, but Eve was more so. This is why Satan approached her rather than him. His tools? "Compliments and adulation." He deluded her innocent heart.

The Greek word translated "innocent" is *akakon.* The elements are *a*, which means "un," or "not," and *kakon*, which means, "evil." Innocence, then, is "not-evil." That is, it is not *about* evil, which is to say, it's naïve—in the best sense of the word. Is naiveté, even in its best sense, a negative trait? In an age of wickedness, yes. People who assume the best of others in this world get chronically hurt and scammed. We cannot fault the intentions of such people, or even their character. It's just that they're unfit— or untutored—in the ways of base society. Isn't it refreshing to meet a truly guileless person? Yes. But would you want such a person negotiating your deal at the used-car dealership?

A man twisting the truth about women once wrote me:

> Men are less emotional and can decide things more rationally. Just as women can be emotional and fickle (especially once a month), thus also mankind is fickle, contradictory, and needs God to be patient with it. In other words, a woman's more emotional nature pictures the fickleness of mankind.

I replied:

> The definition of fickle is, "not constant or loyal in affection." Men are far guiltier of this than women. In Scripture, men are overwhelmingly

preferred by God as examples of disloyalty: Cain, Jacob, the sons of Israel, Laban, David, Solomon, Jonah, the clergy of our Lord's day, and so on. With few exceptions, women are well presented in God's Word: Rebecca, Ruth, Esther, Deborah, the Queen of Sheba, Mary, Martha, Lydia, Priscilla. Men beat Christ; women soothed Him. *Thank you, God, for the rational, emotionally stable men who crucified our Lord and stoned all the prophets.*

What women are once a month, men are 24/7.

Woman is God's picture of why humanity needs God's patience? Not true. God's picture for that is another male: the apostle Paul. Paul writes concerning himself: "But therefore was I shown mercy, that in me, the foremost [sinner], Jesus Christ should be displaying all His patience, for a pattern of those who are about to be believing on Him for life eonian" (1 Timothy 1:16).

We tend to downgrade Eve's innocence by calling it "gullibility." We could do the same with Adam if we were so disposed, calling his distrust of Satan "cynicism." Eve should have believed God, yes, but Satan's wiles overcame her. Simply put, women are unsuited to spiritual warfare. They're too good for it.

"Saved through childbearing"

> Yet she shall be saved through the child bearing, if ever they [that is, Eve's progeny] should be remaining in faith and love and holiness with sanity.

Does this mean that a childless woman disqualifies herself from membership in the body of Christ? Of course not. The question we must ask is: *what is the salvation of the context?* It is not, as commonly supposed, deliverance from death into Christ's kingdom. The context is Eve's role in bringing Adam and the race into sin. Because of this role, women have been stigmatized as lesser beings. The Jews, as a race, suffer similarly for killing Christ. The salvation of the context, then, is a woman's deliverance from this stigma. A woman delivers herself and her gender from Eve's shadow by bringing forth life and then abiding in Christ. Bearing offspring reminds the world that, even though through a woman came sin, through a woman also comes deliverance from sin: Jesus Christ.

Head coverings

In 1 Corinthians 11:1-16, Paul discusses a tradition that he, personally, gave to the Corinthian

church. "Now I am applauding you . . . that you are retaining the traditions according as I give them over to you" (1 Corinthians 11:2). The tradition he's referring to is women praying and prophesying with heads covered. Here's how he explained it:

> Now I want you to be aware that the Head of every man is Christ, yet the head of the woman is the man, yet the Head of Christ is God . . . For a man, indeed, ought not to be covering his head, being inherently the image and glory of God. Yet the woman is the glory of the man. For man is not out of woman, but woman out of man. For, also, man is not created because of the woman, but woman because of the man. Therefore the woman ought to have authority over her head because of the messengers [that is, *angels*].
>
> —*1 Corinthians 11:3,7-10*

Here is how we commonly picture the headship order of 1 Corinthians 11:

God Christ Man Woman

We assume the order of headship in 1 Corinthians 11 to be an order of greatness, from greatest to least, beginning with God. With this assumption, God is the greatest and woman is the least. It is this misapplication that has prompted men to become dictators and women doormats. This is not a greatness issue, however, but an issue of image and glory. Notice: "For a man, indeed, ought not to be covering his head, being inherently the image and glory of God. Yet the woman is the glory of the man."

No one has ever seen the sun with the naked eye. Rather, we see the glory of the sun, that is, the corona. The corona is an image of the sun, not the sun itself. The corona is out of the sun, much as woman is out of man. God, likewise, is invisible, and Christ becomes His glory and image. Through Christ and Christ alone, we see God. Christ comes out of God just as man comes out of Christ, and woman comes out of man, and light comes out of the sun. In 2 Corinthians 4:4 Paul speaks of "the illumination of the evangel of the glory of Christ, Who is the Image of the invisible God."

Continue with the parallel.

Without a husband protecting and nurturing his wife, we lack a modern-day presentation to the world-at-large (and to the angels of heaven) of the sacrifice of Christ (Ephesians 5:25,28). Likewise, without the wife fulfilling her role as the glory of the husband, the best of a man remains hidden. According to Genesis 2:18, woman is man's helper and complement. Question: If woman is man's helper—*then who needs the help?* If woman is man's complement—*then who needs completed?*

"Man is not created because of the woman, but the woman because of the man." This verse is assumed to teach the inferiority of women. However, it teaches just the opposite. Had woman been created first, there would have been no need for man. This is the gist of "man is not created because of the woman." (The cripple is not created because of the crutchmaker, but the crutchmaker because of the cripple. No cripple has ever been created because of a crutchmaker, has he? Equally absurd, then, would be a man created because of a woman.) Again I say: if woman is man's completion, who's incomplete? Woman alone in Eden would apparently not have required completion. Her need of a man comes via the curse, whereas man—post Genesis 2:21—needs woman inherently. Let's probe this further:

And to the woman He said: 'I shall increase, yea increase your grief and the groanings of your preg-

nancy. In grief shall you bear children; yet by your
husband is your restoration and he shall rule over
you.'   —Genesis 3:16, *Concordant Version of
the Old Testament*

The wording of this passage suggests that
a husband rescues his wife from the curse (he
restores her), and that the wife repays the favor
by becoming subservient. As this is misleading,
let's look deeper.

In the Concordant Version, there is a footnote at the word "restoration." The footnote
reads: "Hb impulse." This means that the
Hebrew word here, *teshuqah*, means "impulse,"
not restoration. Why the Concordant Version
put "impulse" in the footnote and not in the
text, I don't know. Additionally, where the word
"over" appears, as in, "he shall rule over you,"
there is a superscript "i," like this: ⁱover. This
means that the word in the original Hebrew
is "in," not over. Again, why the Concordant
Version does not use "in" in the text—is curious
to me. But at least the right words are noted.

Another literal translation of the Hebrew
scriptures, the Dabhar Translation, imports
these elements into the text itself. Here is the
passage from the Dabhar Translation:

Unto the woman He spoke: 'To increase I shall increase your sadness and your pregnancy; in sadness you will bear sons, and unto your man will be your striving, but he, he will rule within you.'

Notice that, for the Hebrew *teshuqah*, the Dabhar Translation has "striving." This is much closer to "impulse" than the Concordant, "restoration." Additionally, there is a footnote at the word "within." The footnote says, "the heart of." Furthermore, where the word "but" appears, as in "but he, he will rule within you," is a superscript "a," like this, ªbut. This means that the word in the original Hebrew is "and," not "but." What does all this mean? The following:

Unto the woman He spoke: 'To increase I shall increase your sadness and your pregnancy; in sadness you will bear sons, *and unto your man will be your impulse and striving, and he, he will rule in your heart.'*

And so, it is not that Adam becomes Eve's restoration. Rather, he becomes her undertaking. It is a newfound void within her—post-curse— that makes her care about Adam in a measure previously unknown. Adam's deficiencies now incline her ("impulse"; "striving") toward his aid. Her heart now tells her that, without her care, this man dies. Remarkably, modern scientific data confirms this. In the longevity department, marriage benefits men more than women, whereas women outlive men no matter their marital status.

Janelle Miles, National Medical Correspondent in Brisbane, Australia, reporting in 2005 for the AAP Newswire, writes:

> Marriage may add almost a year to a man's life, but it does little to boost the lifespan of women, Australian researchers have found. A study of about 3,000 elderly men and women since 1988 found married men lived on average 11 months longer than their single counterparts. But marital status for women made no significant difference to longevity.

In "Journal of Marriage and the Family," Lauren Wispe of the University of Oklahoma writes:

> There is considerable evidence that marriage is positively correlated with longevity for both men and women, although the benefits of marriage favor men more than women. While

matrimony appears to be particularly benevolent to men, the final arbiter, biology, still favors women over men in general mortality rates.

Even after the curse of Eden, men need women more than women need men.

Speaking of general mortality rates, by the age of 100, women outnumber men 8 to 1.

"And he shall rule over you." This mistranslation has wreaked immeasurable societal havoc. No wonder men lord it over women, and husbands over wives; they imagine that God, in Eden, decreed it. What a difference between "he shall rule over you" and "he shall rule *in* you," that is, in your heart. Rather than a warning to women and a command to men, this verse becomes a credit to women and a blessing to men. His welfare is now the burden of her heart. And his sexual clinging—"therefore a man will leave his father and his mother, and will cling unto his woman" (Genesis 2:24, Dabhar Translation)—is the need of her heart. As if a man knows how to rule a woman anyway. Those who foolishly manage it employ intimidation and brute force, that is, violence. Superior strength is a man's only advantage over the fair sex.

Keep in mind that these things, as beneficial as they are (minus the sadness in childbearing),

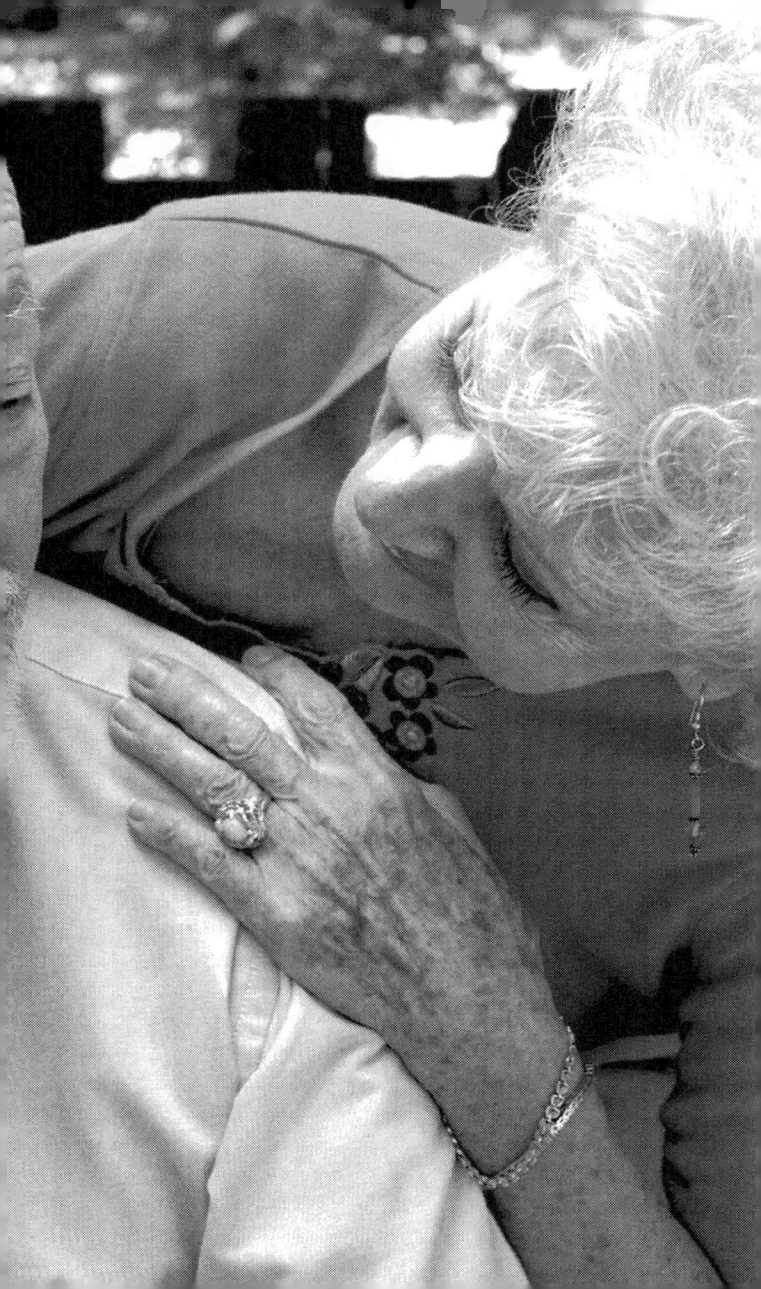

are things that *befell* Eve. They are consequences of sin. Whereas Adam was to cling to his woman from the moment of her creation (Genesis 2:21-24), *before* sin, her impulse and striving is not toward him or altogether receptive of him until after sin's entrance. Remember that 1 Corinthians 11:9—"Man is not created because of the woman, but the woman because of the man"—makes man the lacking one and woman his completion. True, God is the One Who made man to lack, but so be it. Before sin, Eve completed Adam by receiving his clinging. It is only after the entrance of sin that completion, for Adam, became part of Eve's need. She then *wanted* his clinging and sought his welfare. The physical pressing of her husband then became a springboard toward a previously unneeded marvel: emotional oneness.

Tresses

In the marriage covenant, a woman is the glory of the man in that she represents the man to the world-at-large. By extension, she also represents God to the world-at-large. She is to the man what Christ is to God and what light is to the invisible sun: she is his radiance. The husband of the woman of Proverbs 31 is acknowledged in the gateways when he sits with the elders—because of his wife. Because of her, "he lacks no proceeds" (Proverbs 31:11). In addition, "she watches over the affairs of her household" (verse 27). *She* does this, not him.

If a) Christ is the glory of God, and b) man is the glory of God and Christ, and c) woman is the glory of God, Christ and man—then what is the glory of woman? d) Her hair.

I am quite serious. Since woman is the end of the glory road and the most sophisticated creation of God, only something on her person could be *her* glory. It is her hair.

"Is not even nature itself teaching you that if a man, indeed, should have tresses, it is a dishonor to him, yet if a woman should have tresses, *it is her glory*" (1 Corinthians 11:14,15).

Here is how we ought to picture the headship order of 1 Corinthians 11 (contrast this with the illustration on page 46):

GodChristManWoman Tresses

Again, I am as serious as can be. In this graphic representation of headship, that which goes before is the head of the subsequent, yet the subsequent is the glory of that which goes before. Therefore, while God is the head of Christ, Christ is God's glory (His outward shining); while Christ is the head of man, man is

Christ's glory (His outward shining); while man is the head of woman, woman is man's glory (his outward shining); and while a woman is the head of her own hair, her own hair is her glory (her outward shining).

The important thing to note here is that female tresses are last in a list of effulgences (shinings, radiances, glories) that began with God. The conclusion is startling:

A woman's tresses are the world's first contact with the glory of God.

The stars declare God's handiwork, yes, but a woman's hair declares His glory, that is, His beauty. When a woman lets down her tresses, men go numb. They are rendered speechless. Solomon writes of his beloved Shulammite in the Song of Songs: "Your head upon you is like Carmel, and the tresses of your head are like purple: a king is bound by the strands" (7:5). Even the mere strands of this woman's tresses had the power to stop a king in his tracks. Not even other women can take their eyes from the wonder of a woman's cascading locks.

Notice what a complete creation is the woman. To glorify Himself, God creates another being: Christ. To show the glory of Christ comes yet another being: Adam. The glory of Adam requires yet another being: Eve. Eve, being the latest of the creation of God, is so complete that, rather than requiring the creation of another being to glorify her, something on her person fulfills that role: her tresses.

I know how bizarre all this must sound, but we are dealing with a God Who in past eras has used goats, sheep, and the tar that waterproofed the ark to picture His Son. I did not invent this hair revelation; it's 1 Corinthians, chapter 11: A woman's "tresses" (*Concordant Version*) are the glory of the woman, who is the glory of the man, who is the glory of Christ, Who is the glory of God. Thus, by extension, a woman's tresses are the glory of God.

In the realm of humanity, God's glory must begin somewhere. Women instinctively know it's their hair. They spend more money beautifying it than anything else on their person. The next time you're at Wal-Mart, marvel at the rows and rows of women's hair care products. Then, just for fun, try to *find* the men's products.

So why a head covering for a woman, but none for a man? We've been taught that a woman covers her head as a public acknowledgement to all, including the angels (*Concordant Version*, "messengers"), of her husband's headship. This explanation fails on application, however, because note the reason why men are told *not* to cover: 1 Corinthians 11:4, "Every man praying or prophesying having aught on his head, is disgracing his Head." Why would a covered man be disgracing Christ? 1 Corinthians 11:7, "For a man, indeed, ought not to be covering his head, being inherently the image and glory of God."

There is a connection between man and Christ that a covering would symbolically interrupt. It is as if Christ is saying to the man, "I am your Head, your covering, and your protection. By covering your own head, you are symbolically denying My headship. Are you your *own* protection and hiding? How dare you place a layer of protection and hiding between thee and Me."

Protection and hiding is the symbolic purpose of the covering. I'm getting this from verse 15: "Yet if a woman should have tresses, it is her glory, seeing that tresses have been given her instead of clothing." This is the *Concordant Literal New Testament* speaking. When they sinned, Adam and Eve received clothing from God. The clothing served both to hide their newfound shame and to protect them from the elements. Though God gave Adam clothing as well as Eve, Eve already had the covering and protection of her tresses, which functioned as clothing in the pre-sin era. Not so for Adam,

for "if a man, indeed, should have tresses, it is a dishonor to him" (verse 14).

If a man is to be uncovered in recognition of his head, which is Christ, then one would think a woman should also be uncovered in recognition of *her* head, which is man. And yet she covers. Why? Because her covering is not a recognition of her head, but rather a protection and a hiding apart from him.

We have already discussed how it is the mark of a godly, civilized society to cherish and protect its women. Man is automatically protected by his Head, Christ, yet women have been historically abused by their heads. Because of the disparity in physical strength, it is easy for husbands to abuse wives, and men to abuse women in general. Men over the centuries have overreached their headship status and treated women not only as second-class citizens, but as slaves.

Note the disconnect between man and woman that is absent between Christ and man. According to verse 7, man is inherently "the image and glory of God." Yet the second part of the verse says, "the woman is the glory of the man." The difference between the two clauses is that man is the image and glory of God, yet woman is only the glory of man. She is not his image. The man mirrors Christ; the woman mirrors Christ as well—as a part of humanity (Genesis 1:27)—yet in relation to the man, no. She is less like the man than the man is like Christ.

If Christ is a mountain and man the lake that reflects it, then woman is a swan on the lake. This is my concept of the disconnect; the woman belongs to the scene but is distinct from it, covered within the larger covering; apart. Woman beneath man is more her own than man beneath Christ. Man is naked (uncovered) beneath Christ, yet woman, beneath man, has protection. This is Scripture speaking.

Christ we can trust; man—not so much.

"Therefore the woman ought to have authority over her head because of the messengers" (1 Corinthians 11:10).

"Messengers" (*Concordant Literal New Testament*) are angels. The celestial magistrates above us monitor our doings, learning of God and humanity. (For more on this, see my book *Divine Principles of Sexual Attraction*.) In this very letter, Paul himself said, "For we became a theater to the world and to messengers and to humans" (1 Corinthians 4:9). Celestial beings covet a woman covered. They marvel to see females protected. Through this service provided to wives by husbands, the celestial world continually beholds the care of Christ, Who, because of the ecclesia's indifference to Him, could have destroyed it, but instead cherished it.

While the lesson of the head covering changes lives and marriages, the practice is anachronistic. In 1 Corinthians 11:2, Paul calls it a tradition. It was a tradition given over by him to the Corinthian church, suited to the time. Besides being a radically different culture, we have lost the original truth behind the covering. If contemporary women knew the truth, I, myself, could promote it. But it has degenerated into a religious practice. It has degenerated into a badge of pride. The kinds of women who cover today tend to look plain, sad, and surrendered; they pride themselves on how humble they look. This is the opposite of the freed, adored, protected, and died-for woman whose hair is the glory of God. Where, in Scripture, is anyone asked to surrender—let alone a woman to a man? Subjection is another matter.

It is only as wives are protected, cherished, and granted a relative authority beneath the husband's headship that they in turn give joyously of their bodies. When Paul says in 1 Corinthians 7:4 that neither the husband nor the wife has jurisdiction over his or her own body, he assumes the following essentials: 1) the husband adores

"The kinds of women who cover today tend to look plain, sad and surrendered; they pride themselves on how humble they look. This is the opposite of the freed, adored, protected, and died-for woman whose hair is the glory of God."

the wife and nourishes and cherishes her, and 2) the wife receives the adoration, nourishment and cherishing.

"Let the husband render to the wife her due, yet likewise the wife also to the husband" (1 Corinthians 7:3).

Female autonomy

"Therefore a woman ought to have authority over her head" (1 Corinthians 11:10). This verse overturns our preconceptions about head coverings. The woman, not the man, has authority over her head. She is an authority within an authority, autonomous within the larger sphere of government. This is the protection symbolized by both the natural covering (tresses) and the symbolic (head covering).

I am an American and abide by the higher laws of my country. Within this sphere, I am free to do and to be what I will. The best government is a small one, existing to protect my freedoms yet refraining from dictating my life. Thus should a woman be—but rarely is—under the headship of a man. And yet if he will not protect her, God will, not only gifting her with tresses, but symbolically granting her—in His presence—authority over her own self.

Surprisingly, the word "domineer," as in, "I

am not permitting a woman to be domineering over a man" (1 Timothy 2:12) suggests this relative autonomy. The Greek word is *authenteo*, and the elements are "same-be." The definition is, "one who consults himself in his actions toward others." If women are so fragile, dumb, and inept, why does Paul warn them concerning domineering? A prison guard does not tell his prisoner: "I do not allow you to domineer. Consult me before your next decision." Neither does a master tell this to a slave. This warning only fits one either in possession of authoritative gifts and abstaining from their exercise, or exercising them to the full. The potential must exist to lord it over another.

Paul's use of this word in the context of the ecclesia fits the case of "already in possession of authoritative gifts." While the woman is quite able to teach, Paul does not allow her. In the home, however, the woman exercises her gifts to the full—or at least she should. So gifted and proficient is she that the temptation arises to consult none but herself. Many wives need to be reminded that they even *have* husbands.

- She watches over the affairs of her household (Proverbs 31:27)
- I am intending, then, that younger widows

are to be marrying, bearing children, managing the household (1 Timothy 5:14)

In the Proverbs passage above, the word
"watches" is the Hebrew word *tsaphah*. It is
translated "watchman" in Ezekiel 33:7—"And
you, son of humanity, as a watchman (*tsaphah*)
I have given you to the house of Israel. And
when you hear the word from My mouth, then
you warn them from Me." From this we see the
nature and extent of the watching. It involves
not only eyes, but heart, mind, and character. It
operates from a position of God-given authority.

In the passage from 1 Timothy, the phrase
"managing the household" represents a single
Greek word, *oikodespotes*. The elements of
this word are: "home-owner." The root word
for "owner" is *despotes*, from which we derive
our English word, "despot." The definition of
despot is, "one who has absolute possession."
Am I saying that a woman should have absolute possession of her household? The answer is a
guarded, "yes—as long as she consults her head."

Let the wives be subject to their own husbands,
as to the Lord, for the husband is head of the
wife even as Christ is Head of the ecclesia.
                            —*Ephesians 5:22-33*

How does a woman who is subject to a head gain despotism over a household? The same way Joseph gained it under Pharaoh. The ruler says: "You shall rule."

Pharaoh said to his officials: "Shall we find one like this, a man in whom is the spirit of Elohim?" Then Pharaoh said to Joseph: "There is no one so understanding and wise as you. You shall be over my house, and all my people shall obey at your bidding. But in the throne I shall be greater than you." Pharaoh further said to Joseph: "See! I have set you today over all the land of Egypt." Then Pharaoh took off his ring from his hand and put it on Joseph's hand. He had him clothed in garments of cambric, and he placed a decorative chain of gold about his neck. He had him ride in the second chariot that he had; and they called out before him: "Attention!" Thus he was putting him over all the land of Egypt.

—*Genesis 41:38-43*

Pharaoh appointed Joseph over all in Egypt but himself. Yet God requires more of husbands than of Pharaoh. Husbands are to love their wives:

Husbands, be loving your wives according as Christ also loves the ecclesia, and gives Himself up for its sake.

—*Ephesians 5:25*

Pharaoh was never exhorted to love Joseph, or to nurture and care for his soul. But watch this—

Thus, the husbands also ought to be loving their own wives as their own bodies. He who is loving his own wife is loving himself. For no one at any time hates his own flesh, but is nurturing and cherishing it, according as Christ also the ecclesia, for we are members of His body. For this "a man shall leave his father and mother and shall be joined to his wife, and the two shall be one flesh." This secret is great: yet I am saying this as to Christ and as to the ecclesia. Moreover, you also individually, each be loving his own wife thus, as himself, yet that the wife may be fearing the husband.

—*Ephesians 5:28-33*

Pharaoh may have loved, nourished and cherished Joseph, but God never exhorted him to such nobility. Here is something greater. Nourishing and cherishing is the care for another's soul. As a man feeds, protects and comforts his

own body, thus he ought to feed, protect and comfort his wife. Is the husband not still head? He is. But as head in the mold of Christ, he assumes the place of servant and caretaker. He rules her by serving, nourishing and protecting her. He esteems her.

> The husband said to his family: "Shall we find one like this, a woman in whom is the spirit of Elohim?" Then the husband said to the wife: "There is no one so understanding and wise as you. You shall be over my house, and all my people shall heed your bidding. I am the head of the home, and yet I rule by nurturing and cherishing. I rule by serving." The husband further said to the wife: "See! I have set you today over all the household." Then the husband took off his ring from his hand and put it on his wife's hand. He had his wife clothed in the finest garments, and he placed a decorative chain of gold about her neck. He had her ride in his best, newest car, and took the clunker for himself. And when his wife drove the best car, he called out before her: "Attention!" And boy, did all the neighbors pay attention.

In God's unique way of doing things, the master becomes the servant. Appreciate the paradox that a wife's subjection, in the matter of household affairs, can include the laying down of her subjection. One might say that, while a wife remains ultimately subject to her husband, her wisdom—in life's affairs—and his willing acquiescence *to* her wisdom, makes her mistress of the home. Surprisingly, this is the suggestion of Scripture.

In spiritual matters, of course, husbands must lead their wives. I would like to see all husbands exercising a spiritual vision for their families. Women, as we have noted, are the most likely victims of religious seduction. Because of this inherent weakness, husbands ought to exercise a strong hand in leading and keeping their wives in truth. This assumes, of course, that the husband knows truth. If the wife knows truth and the husband does not? She remains subject to him, though without denying her spiritual identity. Here is where her relative autonomy especially applies, that is, in the realm of her God-life.

What about *major* life affairs, such as 1) where to live, 2) finances, and 3) business decisions? I believe that husbands ought to be the visionaries for the future of their wives and families. Husbands ought to lead their wives and families toward better vistas, better places, better lives.

Husbands ought to stand upon and uphold principles of grace, spirit, and freedom in Christ. Within this vision, I prescribe that husbands ought to acquiesce to their wives when possible. Husbands can and should do this without surrendering either their headship or their principles. This is not a sign of weakness, but of respect and conformity to the wife's wisdom. However, Scripture is ever true, "Nevertheless, as the ecclesia is subject to Christ, thus are the wives also to their husbands in everything." The husband is the ultimate decision-maker. Should a clash of wills occur, the wife acquiesces. Contrary to what most men and women assume, this is not a matter of superiority, but of practicality; the husband is not better than the wife. At a major highway intersection, the presence of a "yield" sign makes no comment upon the worthiness of any driver. The overriding concern is preventing crashes and saving lives. Thus also, marriage. And yet, as previously explained, the wise husband yields as he can. Not only this, he—like Pharaoh—gives over the bulk of management to the wiser member, then heeds her word. She thus becomes subject (Scripture is ever true) to her husband's willing (and desired) subjection to her in this area.

Divine paradox

Who made man woman's head in the first place? God did. That seems odd, seeing as how God gave woman more gifts. In God's strange arrangement, however, He blesses the lesser with more responsibility to blend the mix:

> Now our respectable members have no need, but God blends the body together, giving to that which is deficient more exceeding honor, that there may be no schism in the body, but the members may be mutually solicitous for one another.
>
> —*1 Corinthians 12:24-25*

This is similar to making the class trouble-maker responsible for cleaning the erasers. The boy rises to the occasion and becomes a better person.

Whenever I hear men gloating about being the heads of their homes and receiving more exceeding honor, I happily point out that God gives exceeding honor to that which is deficient. Pharaoh was deficient in every way to Joseph, yet still occupied the throne. "Congratulations on your exceeding honor," I say to the husbands. "This proves that you are deficient." It's true. The husbands walk away sulking. I always pray that they swallow their pride and learn how rewarding it is to serve the superior gender.

I continually marvel at God's paradoxes. God gives the lesser sex (males) the headship over the greater sex (females) because in God's odd way of doing business, the deficient (males) get more exceeding honor. And yet, the honor of the deficient (male) is to assume the Christ-like place and serve the more respectable member.

Why didn't God do it "the right way" in the first place and let women lead men without the power struggle? It's called exercise of character. God says: Let us see if man is wise enough to discern the proper direction for marriage (his headship), then bold enough to articulate it. Let us see if woman is humble enough to be taught, then bold enough to live the lesson. Let us see if the husband can trust his wife enough to acknowledge her house-managing wisdom, and the wife faithful enough (and, paradoxically, subject enough) to cherish that which has been entrusted to her.

No one can accuse God of doing things the easy way, yet who can match Him in the personal fulfillment department?

To sum up, men lack the super-clothing afforded women; men are comparatively naked before God and Christ. Within the protection of Christ, we are the vulnerable ones, the expendable half. We see this both in political and spiritual warfare. God would have men die so that women might live. Never, in Scripture, is the converse true. This pictures Christ and His service to the ecclesia, or church.

Women are jewels, and men their temporary caretakers. We will never fully grasp either the elemental mystery of the diadem or its inherent worth. We can only marvel that such a prize is entrusted to us. May God inspire us to embrace this role for ourselves, for God, and for the glory of womanhood. ◆

ZANDER

DIVINE
PRINCIPLES
OF SEXUAL
ATTRACTION

How women are like God
and why men want to
worship them

Everyone knows *how* things are.
This is the only book that tells you *why* they *are*.

EXCERPT
DIVINE PRINCIPLES OF SEXUAL ATTRACTION

The magnetism between men and women is the most powerful, most prolific force on Earth. It is a power that launches armies, shatters kingdoms, and destroys as many lives as it generates. Why is it so ridiculously—*strong?*

Many would say: procreation. Yet God could certainly bring more human beings into the world without, say, spaghetti straps. Or Brut cologne. Or kissing; why the urge to mesh mouths in the first place? What does the exchange of saliva have to do with the transference of seed? And this: does the race perish apart from red roses? Lace-topped stockings?

Satin sheets? I am wondering now about soft music and candlelight. Can we not duplicate ourselves without Ravel's *Boléro?*

I just read a strange sentence on the Internet a few moments ago in an article titled, "Sex After Sixty." A woman whom I will call Mrs. Henderson said: "I did not have my first orgasm until age 84." How can a sentence like this even exist? Is it safe to say that something besides procreation may be occurring here?

Many things less significant than sex and the sun picture divine truth. Jesus set forth lilies and sparrows as parables of God's care. Additionally, when we see a lamb we're to think of Christ's meekness (He called himself, "the Lamb of God"), while the lion calls to mind His strength ("the Lion of Judah").

The apostle Paul picks up a kernel of wheat and says, *Do you people want to know truth?*

Sure, Paul.

Then study a kernel of wheat.

What do you mean?

The apostle holds up the small kernel he has just unearthed. "What you are sowing is not being vivified if it should not be dying" (1 Corinthians 15:36). He shakes his head in utter amazement and then shoves the kernel back into the soil with his big thumb.

If a seed, a lily, a small bird and a lamb picture such monumental truths, what of this power that, second-by-second, rattles the globe? If procreation is this power's fundamental *raison d'etre,* then why is 84 year-old Mrs. Henderson, bless her heart, only now tapping its potency four decades past her childbearing prime?

God could have caused babies to spring up from the ground like corn, or sent them to petitioning humans via the stork. For that matter, He could have made sex clinical: 1) enter procreation booth, 2) draw curtain, 3) insert bolt A into locknut B, 3) wait nine months, and 4) withdraw baby. But no. As with the universe-at-large, moderation is a terrible teacher. God doesn't want it calm and clean. We are sent here to know extremes: desire, denial, longing, and fulfillment. In short, we are sent to find God.

This may explain corsets.

Sexual passion is a parable so high that it dwarfs even the sun and stars in the realm of revelation: *Sexual power pictures for us the drawing power of God. The power of a woman to draw a man is a microcosm of God's ability and intention to return all humanity to Himself.*

We are taught to picture God as an old man with a white beard. No description of Him could be further from the truth; God does not resemble Merlin the Magician. God is not a man, and neither does He resemble one. God Himself is invisible; He is spirit (John 4:24); spirit is His essence. Yet His essence is the most beautiful thing imaginable. We cannot see God, but we behold, day by day, that which has come from Him, that is, His creation.

Notice in Genesis the progressive nature of God's creation. He begins with plants: azalea bushes, sunflowers, wheat, grass, elm trees, and dandelions. He then fills the seas with living, moving souls: plankton, starfish, crabs, scallops, seals, and the giant sperm whale. The sperm whale is a step up from the dandelion—somewhat. The celestial citizens, beholding all this, marvel at God's power.

Without stopping, God then populates the near heavens with various flying things: eagles, hawks, wrens, and the yellow-bellied sapsucker. The sapsucker surely stupefied the celestial worldmights, who no doubt supposed it to be God's *coup de grace*.

They were wrong about that.

Next from God's hand came the life that crawls upon land: ants, porcupines, warthogs, elephants, and cats. Ah, now we have it. Surely with cats God had exhausted His creative genius.

But no.

On day six, God created Adam. As Adam arose from a pile of mud, a hush befell heaven. Before the gaze of all stood a being of reason and wonder, able to kneel and sniff the soil in awe at his own quintessence. *At last, the ceiling.*

Well, not so fast. Surely heaven caught its collective breath as Eve ascended to full height, dressed in a halo of morning mist. What wide, smooth hips. *Her legs! My God! They're longer than the gazelle's!* Birds must have alighted upon her, while butterflies flitted to her hair. The piano had yet to be invented, but whatever celestial instrument prefaced it struck gorgeous tones. For here was not merely another human, but an improved specimen.

In our modern language, Eve was Adam 2.0.

The celestial attendants looked at God, then at Eve; then at God, then at Eve; then at God, then at Eve; God, Eve, God, Eve—on it went. With the thousandth pass, light dawned. Adam mirrored God's strength, but here, in the woman, the celestial world perceived God's crushing beauty.

As did the first man.

Woman is proof, upon the Earth, of the irresistible gorgeousness of God.

> Therefore a man shall forsake his father and his mother and cling to his wife, and they two become one flesh.
>
> —*Genesis 2:23-24*

"God used this small book to change my life. After fifteen years in the pulpit, I finally understand what hell is. Better late than never."
—J. Marcus Oglesby, M.Div.

MARTIN ZENDER
GOES TO HELL

MARTIN ZENDER
Author of "How to Quit Church Without Quitting God"

At last. Here are the facts.

100 pages. Paperback. Available now.
starkehartmann.com Toll Free: 1-866-866-BOOK

A critical look at an uncriticized doctrine.

EXCERPT
MARTIN ZENDER GOES TO HELL

When Adam sinned, what was the conse-
quence? Go and see. Here was the worst
sin ever. What better time to reveal the ultimate,
horrible fate? But it's not there. You'll be driven
from the Garden, Adam, and you'll have to hoe like
mad to make anything grow. Eve, childbearing will
introduce you to pain so severe you'll see white. And
today, you begin to die, both of you. It's the penalty
of your disobedience. Death and weeds and cramps
the color of lightning. And I should mention this as
well—I won't be coming around as often.

Bad enough, but not a word about an eternity of
torture in flames. I wonder why. Do you?

Along comes Cain then, who murders his brother
Abel. Murder is an unknown crime until then, but
the worst since the Satan/Eve/fruit debacle. Now
is a good time for God to unveil the Mother of All
Punishments, to discourage future lawbreakers. But

no, not a word about it. There is judgment, yes, but it's rational and reasonable: Cain's farming labors get cursed—the ground won't produce for him—and he has to wander the Earth as a nomad. We anticipate such phrases as, "Burn forever, murderer," or, "Go to hell, Cain," but they are not here.

I hope no one is disappointed.

What about in the days of Noah? The citizens of that era sinned as a profession. All people thought about back then was: How can we sin with more skill and greater efficiency? They loved their grim occupation and rarely took a break from it. If any people deserved eternal torment, it was these. Burn the blasphemers in hell forever? Surprisingly, no. The sinners merely got wiped out in a flood. Merely? Think about it. One glug and down came your curtain. It couldn't have been pleasant, but it was better than burning forever.

God does sometimes employ fire and brimstone to curtail the careers of professional sinners. Like Lysol, however, fire and brimstone kill germs on contact. (That is, the fire and brimstone do not eternally torment the germs.) Consider the twin cities of Sodom and Gomorrah, cities which today have become synonymous with sexual perversion. When the hour of reckoning arrived, "The Lord rained on Sodom and Gomorrah brimstone and fire from the Lord out of heaven" (Genesis 19:24). The result? God "destroyed the cities of the valley" (verse 29). Note the conspicuous absence of "God began to torment the inhabitants of these cities for eternity."

What about in the days of Moses, when there were laws for everything and a thousand ways to break them? Here's another ideal opportunity for the doctrine of eternal torment to begin "crawling all over Scripture," as I've been told that it is. And yet, it is another opportunity squandered by God and His servant Moses, who could get mad enough to smash rock. All threats in the days of Moses concerned earthly rewards and punishments only. Kill another man's bull, and your bull was killed. Mishandle some point of law, and your crops failed. Tangle with Moses himself, and some terrible thing happened with your wife's hormones. Or an enemy would storm your gates. Or both.

All bad enough, but not crazy. Nothing eternal and not a hint of unending flame. Capital punishment was by stoning then, the worst that could happen. It was nothing you wanted in on, but at least you died. One rock to the head relaxed you enough to dim the finish. No more taxes, tents, scorpions, sand storms, or Moses. For men and women toiling and failing upon an evil planet, death often came as a mercy.

To review, nowhere in the Old Testament does any God-inspired writer mention one word about an eternity of torment for disobeying God. Not one scholar has ever found it, no, not even those who have searched for it desperately. Strange that a doctrine that is "everywhere" has not yet appeared in a segment of the Bible that is, by my reckoning, about three and a half inches thick.

Is it that the amateurs of that delicate era could not shoulder such a responsibility? Then let the Old Testament lightweights stand aside to make way for Someone Who Knows How To Damn. Close the Old Testament books, and make way for genuine terror. Turn one page past Malachi, all ye sinners. To the Gospels! But rejoice not. Rather, fear. For you did not realize how good you had it in the days of old. You are about to pine for those days of flood, famine, and stone. For here, finally, comes One Rising to New Levels of Damnation, a Divine Unveiler of Heretofore Unimaginable Torture. His Good News, in a nutshell, is "Love Me before you die, or my Father will do worse than kill you!" His name?

JESUS CHRIST, SAVIOR.

> The spirit of the Lord is on Me, on account of which He anoints Me to bring the evangel to the poor. He has commissioned Me to heal the crushed heart, to herald to captives a pardon, and to the blind the receiving of sight; to dispatch the oppressed with a pardon, to herald an acceptable year of the Lord...
> —*Jesus Christ, Luke 4:18-19*

Are you ready now to find out how things *really* are?

Pages 35-38

The most frightening threats Jesus made to the Israelites are probably those found in Matthew 5:29-30 and Mark 9:43-48. Here, Jesus explains how much better it is for an Israelite to pluck out his or her eye, or tear off his or her hand, than to let these members lead one into "the fire of hell." These verses have terrified countless millions over the centuries, people to whom the verses don't even apply. These are Israelite threats for an earthly, Israelite kingdom.

The "fire of hell"? That's bad translating. Jesus never said the word "hell" in His life. He didn't speak English. The word that left His lips was *Gehenna*. That's right. Jesus warned the Israelites about "the fire of Gehenna," not hell, and any concordance will confirm this for you (see word #1067 in Strong's, and page 474 in Young's). Gehenna is a small valley along the southwest corner of Jerusalem. It's a geographical location, a place you can walk in today. God made sure that some versions of Scripture got this right (the *Concordant Literal New Testament*, *Rotherham's Emphasized Bible*, and *Young's Literal Translation*, to name three).

As any dictionary will tell you, Gehenna is where the Israelites of old dumped their garbage and offered sacrifices to foreign gods. In the old days it was called the Valley of Hinnom. From *The Random House Dictio-*

nary, under the entry *Gehenna*: "The valley of Hinnom, near Jerusalem, where propitiatory sacrifices were made to Molech." It may be a pleasant green valley today, but in the 1,000-year kingdom it will function as a crematorium for the corpses of criminals (Isaiah 66:23-24).

The "fire of hell"? Here is the only instance where the *King James Version* has taken the name of an actual place and made it something else. Watch this: Where the Greek has *Hierousalem*, the KJV translates "Jerusalem"—every time. Where the Greek has *Nazaret*, the KJV makes it "Nazareth"—every time. Where the Greek has *Bethleem*, the KJV has "Bethlehem"—every time. This is sensible. It's an honorable and consistent way of translating. But here, where Jesus says *Gehenna* (another geographical location), the KJV (as well as the *New International Version*—NIV—and *New American Standard Bible*—NASB), makes it "hell." Gee, that's weird. Can you explain it? I can. Ever hear the phrase, "theological bias"?

Matthew, chapter 25. Here we find "the Son of Mankind come into His glory, seated on the throne." In front of Him are gathered "all the nations," and "He shall be severing them from one another even as a shepherd is severing the sheep from the goats." This judgment is advertised in your local church as "the final judgment" of "all humankind," when "God's enemies" go to either "heaven or hell," for "all eternity." But no. Each sheep and goat represents a nation, not a person. This is not Uncle Harry standing before Jesus; it is Ethiopia. It is not Aunt Hazel trembling before Him; it is Russia. It is not Jim the milkman; it is Afghanistan.

This judgment occurs at the inauguration of the thousand-year kingdom, in the valley of Jehoshaphat. Like Gehenna, this is a literal, geographical location outside Jerusalem (see map again on page 37). As with Gehenna's fire and worms, this judgment is practical. Jesus returns to find Earth's political alignments amok. Good nations will be low; the evil will sit on high. The Great Judge will cure this. What criteria will He use for judging? Their belief in Him? Their confession of faith? The mode of their baptism? No. It will be that nation's policy toward Israel, nothing more. No one will ask, "What church did you go to?" or, "Why didn't you have more faith?"

To make this the general judgment of all humanity is to slaughter the context. But who cares? The possibility of a near-universal twisting of this judgment, and a vast misrepresentation of God's character, will not bother most people. Why? I will tell you. ◆

Dear Martin,
I have just finished *Martin Zender Goes to Hell*. This is one of the best books I have ever read. All anxiety over my loved ones has vanished. Praise God! The facts you present are unassailable. —*Stephen S.*

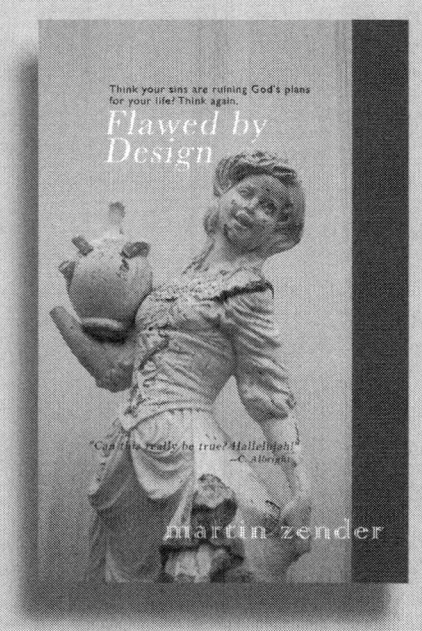

EXCERPT
FLAWED BY DESIGN

Pages 11-13

A woman crashes into the home of Simon the Pharisee. The town sinner, she neither knocks nor removes her sandals. Whoredom is fresh on her clothes, yet something belying this rests angelically upon her face. Only one person here can appreciate the transformation. The woman hurries to the feet of the Master.

An unusual thing had occurred in the early morning hours of that day, after the last man (the last client) had slipped into the Jerusalem night. As she looked about her cubicle, a dread of the future gripped her. Why should she feel this now? Why tonight? No immediate answer came, yet a vision of her final hours flickered in the flame of her one remaining candle. She would die in this room; which night, she did not know. It would be soon, though. Death would come slowly in a pool of blood, released onto the floor by her own hand. Her sister

Mariba would find her. Mariba would scream, there would be a funeral—thirty days of mourning—then it would all be over.

The walls closed in. Stars twinkled outside these walls, somewhere. A sun shone on the other side of Earth, though not for her. For her there was only the shadow cast by her burning piece of wax, a leather ghost running from her feet to a corner, up a wall, across the ceiling, then back to her naked feet. Nothing could escape the cubicle. Floor, wall, ceiling, then back to engulf her. Her hands went to her face now; she was crying.

She had to get out.

Not one other soul occupied the side street where she burst from her home. Urgency along this void of humanity became her silent scream. She would not break down in the city.

Outside the Essene gate, down the valley of Hinnom, up over the aqueduct, then west toward the Bethlehem Road; this brought her to the field. Recently gleaned, dead and quiet, the soil sent coolness into her legs. From above, the heavens lay frozen and mute. Between these two voids she fell to her knees to gather a piece of Earth. Instead, she found a stone, for God had placed it there centuries ago, for her to find. Now it would become her means of hating Him. She picked up the stone as a man would grasp it, then found her feet. Her left eye was already trained into the heavens, right wrist cocked toward the throne room.

All agonies now shifted to the act of throwing. Every sinew, muscle, joint, and fragment of despair made ready the rock for the face of God. She would hit Him, yes. And her tongue, too, lay poised with the forbidden question, "What have You *made* me?!"

The stone traveled a little way into space, propelled by the impetus of the word "made." But then it returned to Earth, though she never heard where.

She had missed.

The forbidden question, however, had not missed at all. In fact, it had hit squarely, and she knew it. Something had happened. Now she felt millions of invisible eyes. She had unmistakably commanded something, perhaps everything. The field was now a stage. With knowledge of this came a liberating rush of boldness. What happened next happened too quickly to stop.

Pages 29-30

Frustrated with your failures? Feeling condemned? Can't overcome a bad habit? I've got great news for you:

"Now we have this treasure in earthen vessels, that the transcendence of the power may be of God and not of us" (2 Corinthians 4:7).

Your humble little vessel of sin is made that way on purpose. We are clay pots by design, not because we have gone afoul of God's intention for us. Let this revelation soothe the exhausted self-improver. Retire, Christian soldier! You fail by design, not because you are a failure. God wants you cognizant of the source of your power, and He has many creative ways of driving this home. One of these is sin.

Wouldn't some of us love to shed our earthenware now and still walk among mortals? Our sins keep us from producing a perfect walk, and we mourn this. What we do not understand is that an imperfect walk is the main idea of this life. God puts the treasure of His spirit in earthen vessels now to keep the vessels from situating themselves upon high places. A perfect walk is not what we need right now. Who could live with us? Could we stand ourselves? Humility is a blessed thing this side of resurrection. Vessels on high shelves sit poised, ready to topple and shatter upon hard floors. Pride is burdensome and is known for preceding falls. Can it be so bad to be delivered of this?

Thank God for the comfort of mistakes. Mistakes remind us of our clayhood and drive us toward Christ. When we finally quit chasing perfection and accept these vessels of clay, we will become happier. When we forget about ourselves, peace will ensue. The happy acceptance of imperfection is the beginning of easy breathing. Because, really, how can you be peaceful and flogging yourself simultaneously? You can't. That's why no one in a religion is truly happy.

People in religions act happy because they're expected to, but they're only one step away from disappointing their deity and suffering his wrath. How happy can they truly be?

Pages 34-36

In the Bible, God is always getting humans into scrapes so that He can get them out of the scrapes and show His power. You say, "No, Martin. God isn't getting the humans into the scrapes. The humans are getting themselves into the scrapes." Well, that theory works fine until you consider accounts such as the hardening of Pharaoh's heart. And we're going to do that shortly. But first I want to show you how God delights in making things humanly impossible before He sets to work.

Remember the story of the blind man Christ healed? What is the first thing the Lord does? He spits on the ground, makes mud, and then smears the mud on the man's eyes. Then He tells the man to go wash in the Pool of Siloam. The guy comes back reading *The Jerusalem Post*. Just when you think God is crazy with this mud business, you start to wonder, *Maybe God is making a point. Maybe mud on top of blindness is God's way of compounding a problem.*

Consider 1 Kings, chapter 18, when Elijah challenged the prophets of the false god Baal to a contest, to see which God was real. Elijah and the prophets of

Baal would each set up an altar. Each would pray to their God to send fire down to their respective altars. The God who sent fire down would be the true God. The prophets of Baal went first.

According to verse 26 of that chapter, the prophets of Baal "called on the name of Baal from morning until noon, saying, 'O Baal, answer us.' But there was no voice and no one answered. And they leaped about the altar which they made."

No Baal. It was Elijah's turn.

Notice the curious thing Elijah does to his altar. I'm quoting from verses 33-35. Elijah said, "'Fill four pitchers with water and pour it on the burnt offering and on the wood.' And he said, 'Do it a second time,' and they did it a second time. And he said, 'Do it a third time,' and they did it a third time. And the water flowed around the altar, and he also filled the trench with water.'"

With the dousing of the altar, Elijah, through the spirit of God, was setting up a field of "impossibility" on which God would demonstrate His power.

Is God making some things impossible for you? Is God dousing your life with water? And when you seem about to recover, is He dousing you a second time? Then a third time? Is there running water in the trenches of your life? Are you getting ready to put on your swimsuit, sit down, and stare at your insurmountable trials? Good. The sooner you do that, the better off you'll be. God has purposely dampened your life with impossibilities, in order to bring you to the end of yourself. The result is that you will be in a relaxed position (flat on your back, for instance, or on your face) to hear and see His new plan for your life. ◆

Martin,

   I heard you on a radio show in Chattanooga, TN about a year ago. You debated a Baptist minister. The host sent me one of your books: *Flawed by Design*. I had been a Baptist from a young age until about twenty. Then there were too many questions that didn't add up, so I became mostly an atheist.

   When I read your book, I nearly went deaf because of all the clicking sounds. Those were the sounds of all those things in the Bible that didn't add up, clicking into place. I credit your book as the means God used to allow faith in Him to return to me. I now realize that Christ died on the cross for all our sins and His grace is sufficient to save us.   —*John P.*

Beyond Politics
What to do while we're here

martin zender

EXCERPT
BEYOND POLITICS

According to the apostle Paul in 2 Timothy, chapter three, in the last days perilous periods will be present and nothing is going to stop them, not even Republicans. Anyone supposing that in the last days humanity will perfect itself is thinking his or her own pleasant thoughts and is out of tune with the mind of God. Our Lord Jesus Christ is not returning to Earth to congratulate us on a job well done. He is coming to sweep away the perilous periods and establish something that we have never seen before: righteous government. And so—

"Cease striving and know that I am God...I will be exalted in the earth" (Psalm 46:10).

"God's indignation is being revealed from heaven on all the irreverence and injustice of humans" (Romans 1:18).

God has promised to take care of the irreverent and unjust, but He will do it in His time, not in ours. Jesus chided Peter for taking up the sword in Gethsemane, saying, "Are you supposing that I am not able to entreat My Father, and at present He will station by My side more than twelve legions of messengers? How, then, may the scriptures be fulfilled, seeing that thus it must occur?" (Matthew 26:53-54). It's the same situation today. Few understand today that God is able, at any time, to reveal His indignation on irreverence and injustice. I have to remind myself of this all the time. The fact that He has not yet moved to impress upon Earth's inhabitants His power means only one thing: it's not yet time for it. When the hour does arrive, God will turn the sun black, make the stars fall, roll up the heavens, move islands, burn up thirty-three percent of the earth, and turn a third of the sea into blood (Revelation 6:12-14, 8:7-8).

I guess that will be impressive enough.

Not only is it wrong to worry about the moral downslide of America and its leaders (Philippians 4:6), but no slave of the Lord will be found fighting it (2

Timothy 2:24). A decline must take place (2 Timothy 3:1-9, Daniel 12:9-10), and happy is the soul taking refuge in God until destruction passes by (Psalm 57:1). Concerning those vessels of dishonor destined to carry out the end-time decadence (Romans 9:21-23, Proverbs 16:4, Revelation 22:11), Paul's advice to believers is to shun them (2 Timothy 3:6), not fight or reform them. It is not ours to be judging those who are outside. "Now those outside, God is judging" (1 Corinthians 5:13).

God is the One Who is operating all in accord with the counsel of His will (Ephesians 1:11). For those of you who do want to cease striving but have been intimidated out of it by your politically active Christian friends, may this book provide your long-sought Scriptural grounds for minding things above (the heavenly kingdom), not things on earth.

Concerning national defense, I am not so pie-in-the-sky that I think we should write national policy based on trust. I wish that we could, but the eon in which we live is naughty, not nice. It's a wicked eon (Galatians 1:4), and thus it is naïve for us to think that we can sit down and negotiate with sinister entities. Neville Chamberlain tried that with Hitler, and it did not end so well. We ended up ditching Chamberlain and bombing the crap out of Hitler. In a wicked eon, we need a strong military. I am proud of our soldiers, and thankful for them.

I'm speaking of national policy now, and not the policy of individuals. I am not personally going to chase down evil dictators; I'm afraid I would catch them. But I think it's good for our armed forces to do so; they *want* to catch them, and should. We must protect our homeland. If an evil dictator entered my literal house and threatened my family, I would stab him repeatedly with a screwdriver. (I don't own a gun. I'm all for gun-owning, I just don't like loud noises.)

An evil dictator striding through my kitchen is a microcosm of an army entering our fair land. It is a natural instinct to protect loved ones as long as it's not too noisy. And yet an individual believer may choose the path of non-resistance, which is the most excellent path. I'll be talking about that later—about whether or not we should be subject to evil governments.

People tell me that I have to know what's going on in the world. I say, "show me the verse." It's fascinating, but no one has yet shown me the verse. If there were such a verse, I am convinced that I would have been shown it by now. I have not taken a newspaper, ever. People have said to me, "Why don't you get the paper, Zender?" and my stock answer is, "Because I might find out what's happening in the world." I don't understand how people can read newspapers and live to tell about it. Well, they generally don't live. They get cancer and die. It takes a little time to die of worry, but it happens eventually.

Reading newspapers is the very definition of minding things of the earth. It's like going to a restaurant and saying, "Give me your War Special and a side order of Worry. For dessert, I would like a large Plane Crash and a Communist Coup." Good God. What do you expect? How can you expect peace when you order an entrée of War? I am not even mentioning the 11:00 news, but don't get me started. Oh, it's too late. "Honey. Turn on the news. Let's watch colorful, hi-definition accounts of kidnappings, rapes, racial discord, house fires, and tsunamis in faraway places. Then we'll go nite-nite." ◆

martin zender

The book for people with weaknesses

HOW TO BE FREE FROM SIN WHILE SMOKING A CIGARETTE

EXCERPT
HOW TO BE FREE FROM SIN WHILE SMOKING A CIGARETTE

Pages 11-13

I don't smoke, but I sometimes wish I did. I have other questionable habits that I won't burden you with. But I can picture myself holding a cigarette, or letting it hang cockeyed out of my mouth like Humphrey Bogart used to do. Whenever I talked—mumbled, I mean—the cigarette would bounce up and down. Then I'd squint and say something devilish to Lauren Bacall.

In this fantasy of mine, I know smoking is bad for me. I know it's wrong. I know I'm sinning, even while I'm doing it. But I do it anyway because it's cool, because life has been unfair to me, because Bacall has great legs, and because if I don't do *something*, I'll lose my mind. It's the worse kind of sin: knowing it's bad, but doing it anyway.

Preachers today lower their voices when speaking of such badness. They'll talk all sing-songy about stock sins like anger, jealousy, and pride. I call these stock sins because they're a dime a dozen. I'm not saying they're not bad, but I find myself doing them without even thinking. The sins I'm talking about—the sins that make the preachers furrow their eyebrows and talk like Vincent Price—are the ones where the wretched sinner says, "Yes, this would be a sin, all right," then does it anyway.

According to the clergy, there's no refuge for this. It's not like it's an accidental sin. It's not like it's a one-time deal. It's more like, "We're sorry, Lord, for what we did today. And we're sorry, too, that we're probably going to do it again tomorrow. And the day after that. And the day after that." The only comfort from the pulpit for this kind of badness is the remote possibility of a Sno-cone stand in hell. So no matter what your particular weakness is—

Well, hold on a minute. It just occurred to me that maybe you don't have a weakness. This is something I had not considered until now, and it changes everything. This project is shot if most of my readers don't have a weakness. If you don't have a weakness, how can I let you waste your time reading a book about weaknesses and how to deal with them? If you don't have a weakness, then please accept my apology, return this book to your bookseller, and use the money you saved to send a real sinner to Bible camp.

This book is written only for those who know what they're supposed to do but sometimes don't do it. It's written for those who think that their own particular weakness keeps God from completely liking them. It's written for those who just can't shake a bad habit. This book is written for the wretched souls who totter between their passion life and their desire for God, not realizing that in order to have a desire for God they must also be dogged by at least one nagging passion that keeps them humble and needing Him. It was wrong of me to assume the worst of you. So forgive me, please, and have a blessed day.

For those who do have a weakness—or two— welcome to paragraph seven. It appears that we've lost a few of the religious folks. At least now we can speak honestly among ourselves.

We're believers. Or we're seekers. Some of us love Jesus Christ already; others aren't sure if we want to or not. In either case, there are bad things we all do occasionally (or continually, perhaps) that dismantle our happiness in front of God. They've got a term for this dismantling that is so weighty and terrible it deserves its own paragraph.

The term is guilt.

Is it possible to be free from sin, even while sinning? Is it possible to be free from sin and the guilt associated with it, even while narrowing your eyes at Bacall and leaning toward her match?

I know what religion has told you. Religion has told you that freedom from sin means you don't sin anymore. But is this God's thought? If this is God's thought, then no one today can be free from sin—at least none of the honest people who made it past paragraph six. But I generally find that God's thoughts and the thoughts of orthodox religion are two different things. I'm happy to report it's also the case here.

This book is written and dedicated to all the poor sinners in the world who can't stop sinning, but who love or want to love the Lord, Jesus Christ. Here's the good news: *You have already been freed from sin.*

Thanks for hanging on. God's Word is about to deliver you from discouragement, condemnation and guilt, without asking you to change a thing you're doing. On second thought, you may have to change one thing. If you've been beating yourself over the head trying not to sin, you're going to have to quit that. Stop assaulting your head.

You still here? Great. That last paragraph wasn't a joke. I would never joke about something as serious as sin. How could I possibly tell you to quit pummeling yourself over it? Because this monumental effort—and the repeated failures and inevitable guilt trips that follow—is ruining your opinion of yourself, taking away your peace, and robbing you of the affection due Christ. You're working so hard trying to *impress* Him that you're not paying enough attention *to* Him.

"But if I let down my guard for even a second," you say, "I'll sin like a crazy person."

Hold on. That's what religion has told you, and I just suggested that religion is usually wrong. It's wrong here, for sure. Religion supposes that by keeping a moral watchdog chained to your flesh, you'll stop sinning. You've probably already disproved this theory with many a botched New Year's resolution. The Pharisees disproved it 2,000 years ago.

Pages 19-20

Before his trial, Scripture describes Job as "flawless and upright." This is verse 1 of chapter 1. But then Job loses his family, his wealth, and his health. Now listen to him in chapter 10, verse 1: "My soul is disgusted with my life; let me give free rein to myself and my concern; let me speak in the bitterness of my soul." Ah, there's the real Job, the mess of a man that was seething beneath that skin all along. But before he could understand his weakness, Job had to be broken. Can you imagine your Christian brother or sister even thinking Job's "blasphemous" words? No one would invite the real Job to the Wednesday prayer meeting, at least not without asking him to comb his hair and keep his scabby mouth shut.

George Bernard Shaw was a genius. It was he who said: "Virtue is insufficient temptation." Many times, those who appear virtuous have not been sufficiently tempted. Their virtue is Hollywood-wall virtue, propped up with half a dozen two-by-fours and a New Year's resolution. It's self-control untested. The world can spot phony Christian virtue ten miles away. Christians can't see it because they are too busy admiring themselves in the mirror.

Real human virtue is being broken by trial and lying like a pile of lumber in the wake of a hurricane. That's when the good stuff starts; it's when God goes to work. Real human virtue is helplessness before God. Helplessness before God is the beginning of a true spirituality that stands strong when the wind blows. Well, it has no place to go but up.

Romans 5:8—"Yet God is commending this love of His to us, seeing that, while we are still sinners, Christ died for our sakes."

God went out of His way here to say, in effect, "I did not justify you in your Sunday clothes. I did not justify you while you were loving your neighbor as yourself, or praying to Me in the quietness of your room. Instead, I justified you while you were yelling at your children, running up your credit card, stuffing yourself with donuts—and worse. I did this for you on your worst day, not your best. I did it this way so that you could thank Me the rest of your life instead of wasting your time trying to figure out how to downplay your faults and impress Me."

What did you say, God? Our robes were rustling.

When God justifies us this way, we're finished before we start. Since He did His best for us at our worst, what can we do now to improve the relationship? Act better? But He already did His best for us while we were acting our worst. What can we do now to blow our relationship with Him? Sin? But He already maxed out on His love for us while we were sinning like crazy people. ◆

Dear Martin,
I stumbled across your book at the library while researching other faiths and was instantly intrigued. As I read, I could literally feel the guilt falling off of me. I swear I feel 10 pounds lighter each day because I no longer pack my sins around with me. I feel the love of God more clearly now than ever. The reality of God's grace is beautiful. The pure logic of it is so obvious now, but was so hidden before. Thanks be to Him, and to you for voicing it. The only regret I have is that it took so long for me to truly experience the power of the cross. —Susan R.

"A provocative, intellectual romp.
You need to read this book!"
~Dwight Green
Ft. Worth Star-Telegram

martin zender

HOW TO
QUIT CHURCH
WITHOUT
QUITTING GOD

Why going to church today is
unbiblical, un-Christlike, and
spiritually risky.

How to Quit Church Without Quitting God

"Confronting hypocrisy, contradiction, and cult overtones in modern-day Christianity head-on, Zender raises serious criticisms without renouncing true faith. A truly fascinating book, and compelling reading for faithful churchgoers and disillusioned church members alike."

Michael J. Carson
The Midwest Book Review

"Zender's book will no doubt cause great irritation to clergy members everywhere. But it's only because no one has had the courage to state ideas as critical as his."

Dan Julian
The State News

"Zender's conversational writing style turns discussion about strict religious dogma into a fun-filled frolic. Although vehemently spiritual, he is the Robin Williams of the roadside tent revival. It is a provocative, intellectual romp through the Bible basics."

Dwight Greene
Fort Worth Star-Telegram

"Zender writes in such an informed, entertaining, and challenging way that one experiences a whole series of epiphanies as they make their way through this delightful look at how religion works in our lives."

Alan Caruba
Bookviews

"Reading Zender makes you laugh, gets you mad, and starts you to thinking. His snappy, in-your-face writing grabs you as he forcefully tackles hypocrisy that masquerades as religion."

Chris Meehan
The Kalamazoo Gazette

"An excellent book that is part of what are probably the three best books on the problems of the church today."

Harold McFarland
Readers Preference Reviews

EXCERPT
HOW TO QUIT CHURCH
WITHOUT QUITTING GOD

This book describes the joy and freedom you will experience by quitting organized religion. By necessity, it must expose the world's most popular religion, and the hypocrisies that poison it. The way I see it, no one can properly enjoy God from the perspective of an institution. But who will quit the institution if they think that everything is "just fine" there? But nothing is "just fine" there, not even close. So I sound the call to freedom. I do this, not by promoting my own authority or instructing you from my podium (the method of most "how-to" authors), but by pointing out the spiders on the institution walls and demonstrating how green (and pest-free) is the grass on the other side.

I believe one of the main reasons the world rejects Jesus Christ is that it thinks He's a member of the religion bearing His name. If only the world realized how much Jesus hates hypocrisy, ice-cream socials and repetitive worship songs, they would depart without compunction. I saw a bumper sticker recently that said, "I have no problem with God, it's His fan club I can't stand."

Millions of church people today secretly want to quit church, but they balk because they think that if they quit church, they'll be quitting God. No. God and His Son quit organized religion years ago, and haven't been back. (Well, they never were members in the first place.) And would you believe me if I told you that not one person in the Bible ever "went to church"? The church is a people, not an address on Main Street. One does not *go* to it, one *is* it.

Do you go to church every week? Then this book will challenge you. Have you walked away from organized religion? Then this book will comfort you. Have you avoided religion all your life?

You may be a spiritual genius. ◆

EXCERPT
THE FIRST IDIOT IN HEAVEN

From the back cover

While on Earth, Jesus said some difficult things. He told the rich to give away all their money, and the joyful to become mourners. If you wanted to inherit the Earth, you had to be meek. If your eye offended you, no problem—as long as you plucked it out. A friend of mine said, "Can I start following Jesus on Monday? I'd like to enjoy the weekend."

The words and commandments of Jesus are pure, perfect, holy—and meant for Israelites. Jesus Himself said, "I was not sent except to the lost sheep of the house of Israel" (Matthew 15:24).

Is it possible that we have been struggling along someone else's path? What if the words in red were never meant to be our marching orders?

Several months after leaving Earth, the Jewish Messiah appeared as a very non-Jewish light to a self-righteous idiot en route to Damascus to kill Christians. Up next? Not only a startling new destiny for believers (heaven instead of Earth) but a new message of pure grace for all humanity.

This is that story.

Pages 15-16

You want to live like Jesus, you really do. You're sincere as can be, but it's an uphill climb. You love people and you love God, so maybe today will be the day you can finally imitate His Son. Maybe today you can finally be meek, turn the other cheek, and rejoice while getting mud thrown in your face.

Think how good it would feel to be pure—to have no sin and no guilt. Think how good it would feel to wake up calm each morning, love everyone during the day, and rest your head at night with a prayer for your enemies.

If only.

And yet it never quite works out that way. In the darkness of your bed each night, you know who you are. Jesus was Jesus, but you are you. When you curl up beneath the covers, you face the terrible truth: It has been another day of failure and frustration.

If only there were a gospel in the Bible for common, ordinary human beings. Or even mediocre people. It seems the gospel of Jesus that tells us to live like Jesus sets the bar just a little too, um, *high*.

I know all about it. I was raised Catholic. The

nuns told me all I had to do was be meek and mild like Jesus (plus do everything else like Jesus) and I would go to heaven. It seemed like a tall order for someone with cartoons on his underpants. What did I know? All I wanted was to play football and eat candy.

Pages 18-19

Why do we have such a difficult time shaping up and producing fruit worthy of repentance? Maybe better to ask: Why do we instinctively know that we *can't* do these things? Why do we give up *trying* to do them? Is it because we are lazy? Ungodly? Satanic? Because we think we deserve nothing more than to be crushed beneath God's fist? Or could it be that, deep down, we think God doesn't really expect us to weep and wail, repent, and be practically perfect in every way? But if He doesn't expect all that, what do we do with all the Bible verses saying that He does expect it? Could it be there are *other* Bible verses that say *different* things?

Are you bold enough to entertain a new thought? What if we, who are not Israelites, have a different gospel—*in the Bible*—than the one meant for Israel? What if this other gospel even has a different name? What if it has a different set of requirements (and a different outlook on run-of-the-mill people or hapless nincompoops) than the gospel given to Israel?

And—think of this—what if this gospel promises an enormously better destiny than the one promised to Jewish believers?

Were faithful Israelites ever promised heaven? Not once. Jesus Himself said, "The meek shall inherit the Earth" (Matthew 5:5). Wouldn't Jesus have known what He was talking about? Israelites never dreamed of getting lifted from Terra Firma. Why would they? Jesus never spoke to them of such a thing. And neither did their prophets. Faithful Israelites were promised that they would rule and reign over the other nations of Earth. This was the promise God made to Abraham.

Back to my question. What if this different gospel I have been referring to (the easier one; the kinder and gentler one; the one that caters to those of us who are not-so-perfect) *does* take people to heaven? Wouldn't that be mind-boggling? It would mean that the nuns at my school were all wrong. Imitating the walk of Jesus would not have gotten me to heaven—as they insisted it would—but would, instead, have kept me on Earth to rule the other nations. What *would* get me to heaven would be giving up trying to be like Jesus and embracing a gospel for regular folks—assuming such a gospel actually exists.

Wouldn't that be something God would do? Bless the socks off average, ordinary people? Doesn't it align with everything we know about His penchant to stun loser-types (fishermen, prostitutes, tax-collectors) with draughts of favor? So God gives reformed sinners (obedient Israelites) what He promised them—namely, Earth—but then later announces a *different* gospel that seats unworthy people (those who haven't a prayer of being like His Son) at His right hand in the highest regions of heaven.

Would this be a gospel you'd like to learn about? ◆

Just finished my first reading of *The First Idiot in Heaven*. I had never heard of Martin Zender, or this message. I am astounded! I had begun to think something was wrong with me. That perhaps God wasn't interested in me. That I was simply not invited to be in His family. I could not figure out why I could not understand either the bible or what my church taught. God knows how desperately I've wanted to. It is as though scales have been lifted from my eyes! I HAVE PRAYED FOR THAT SO MANY TIMES. I can't wait to learn more and my heart is crying out to be a herald. Thank you, Lord God, and thanks to Mr Zender!   —*Gordon S.*

READER COMMENTS:
The First Idiot in Heaven

"Martin, What can I say? Wow! Thank-you. I just ordered a bunch of *First Idiots* to give to friends who love wisdom, humor, and revelation. Everything was laid out just right, and succinct. Paul himself would be amazed. Thank you for not giving up your calling." —Kathy K.

"Hi Martin. I'm having a book while reading your beer! It's very, very good, but you've gotta know: They're gonna kill you for this one Zender ;) Love your work! Grace and peace from Norway!" —Erik S.

"I have been a Zender fan since his first book took the scum off of my eyes 15 years ago and gave me great peace. This book is a continuation of that peace. I can only say: Thanks, Martin. Were it not for you and your books, I would be truly confused and lost in a man-made religion." —Bud M.

"Wow! Just finished *The First Idiot in Heaven*, and I think it is your best book yet. That's a big deal, since the others were so excellent. I hated to see the pages count down to 0." —James F.

"A must-read. The Evangel entrusted to Paul is so beautiful when contrasted with the Circumcision gospel. This book clearly differenciates the two. My prayer is that Father opens many hearts to *The First Idiot in Heaven*. This is a classic Zender book to be read and reread." —Max P.

"Best Zender book ever! (That's saying a lot.) I love the delivery, the humor, the wisdom. From the moment I picked up this book, I only put it down to go to work. Instant classic." —Darron H.

"Written with such clarity. Liberating, and nearly effortless to understand. No more anguish, guilt, shame. Martin, THANK YOU." —Susan L.

"This is the methodical, Scripturally-backed work I've always longed for. My deepest questions are answered. An articulate illustration of the difference between the writings of Paul and the rest of the Bible. Clearly, Martin's most powerful book to date." —Jana L.

"OMG!" —Cynthia F.

www.youtube.com/zendermeister

The
MARTINZENDER
DANSHERIDAN
Show

WBRI
indianapolis

www.martinzender.com

My husband, 2 grown sons and I have been listening to your daily messages for a couple of years now. You are refreshingly different. I've been on a search for truth for about 10 years. We listened to a variety of Internet messages but settled on yours because it's dependable, funny, and best of all is NOT like regular church teaching. The gift you've been given is clarity. It's not a commonly possessed gift! —*M.R., Atlanta*

Dear Martin, Please keep the Clanging Gong News coming! We are a couple of families living in eastern Iowa, and have been getting together for fellowship for a few years now. You are a breath of fresh air to us! I have been known to read sections of your newsletter out loud, with tears in my eyes. God put you in our lives at exactly the right time. Keep doing what you do! —A.B., *Cedar Rapids*